TESTIMONIALS

JOHN FRASER Director of Education, Peel Region, Retired
"Never, in 15 years as Director of the fourth largest school board in Canada, have I encountered a person who is more intelligent, insightful, creative, generous, and with such a commitment to improve education for all, than Diane Devenyi."

LINDSAY ANDREOTTI Chief Experience Officer, Earth. University
"When it comes to imagining how education could be for our future generations, no one is more passionate and curious as Diane. This book will undoubtedly shift the skills of parents and teachers who genuinely want their kids to succeed in life. **Our kids need this** and it's time to let them all be their true genius!"

DR. RENIA TYMINSKI Director, Hallowell Gardens, Centre for Listening and Lifelong Learning
"Dear Genius addresses some fundamental issues that can have a lifelong impact on both mother-tongue English speakers and second language learners. This has resulted in **a book that every parent and teacher needs to read."**

DR. JACKIE ELDRIDGE Lecturer: Master of Teaching Program Curriculum, OISE (Ontario Institute for Studies in Education)
"Diane is one of the most passionate educational professionals I have met. Her unique program is designed to offer an alternate approach to improving skills that have been missed in the learning journey. All learners must have the opportunity to learn in whatever way works for them and Diane is ensuring this prospect for all."

MARGOT LEVITT Retired Elementary School Teacher
"Diane has managed to capture the frustration and pain of students who do not "progress as expected." This book reassures students as well as parents and teachers that the student is not stupid or unteachable. As students develop certainty of the alphabet, their confidence grows and they internalize that **successful reading and writing has nothing to do with being smart and everything to do with being taught smartly."**

Dear Genius,

Harness the Hidden Power in Your ABCs

for neater writing, better spelling,

faster reading and

turning thoughts into words

Diane Devenyi

ISBN: 978-1-7772843-4-3
First Edition
Printed in Canada
Published by The Learning Force Inc.

WELCOME, GENIUS!

In this book you'll find answers to a number of questions you may have about literacy.

Some relate to challenges you may have encountered when learning to read and write, such as:

1. Why did I struggle to read and write with traditional teaching methods?

2. What does it mean when I have messy writing, poor spelling, slow reading, inconsistent focus, or trouble turning thoughts into spoken or written language?

3. Is it too late for me to improve?

4. How do I build or re-build the strongest foundation for learning to read and write in English?

Even if your interest lies only in question 4, I encourage you to read the entire book. You'll first see how gaps can occur with an incomplete literacy education, and the impact these gaps can have. Then, you'll learn that there's a way to build a new solid foundation that can both prevent and fill in gaps, wherever you are in your literacy journey.

DEDICATION

I dedicate this book to the mis-diagnosed, the mis-understood and the simply "missed." Could this be you?

Or do you care about that person?
I see you. I am you.

You're in the right place — wherever you are.

Today's the day to take one small step toward your new story — as you read about others who once lived your story. And for whom everything shifted. It can for you as well.

You're about to learn new ideas that may surprise you. And more importantly, they will spark hope.

As you read on, I ask one small favour:
Read the promise below ... then give it life.

"I promise to direct my energy
toward finding ways to apply this new information
for my benefit and the benefit of those I care about."

To you on your journey — Diane

"Each second we live is a new and unique moment of the
universe, a moment that will never be again.
And what do we teach our children?
We teach them that two and two make four,
and that Paris is the capital of France.
When will we also teach them what they are?
We should say to each of them:
Do you know what you are?
You are a marvel. You are unique.
In all the years that have passed,
there has never been another child like you.
Your legs, your arms, your clever fingers,
the way you move...
You have the capacity for anything.
Yes, you are a marvel.
You must work,
we all must work,
to make the world worthy of its children."

— Pablo Casals,
Catalonian Cellist, Composer and Conductor

Acknowledgements

Thank you for your interest in a topic that's near and dear to my heart: how to support access to literacy for those historically left out by a system that seeks uniformity.

Here's to those who learn and think differently.

And here's to the parents who keep searching for ways to support their children. You have inspired me to find positive answers to troubling questions about learning differences and offer hope of brighter futures for those previously left behind.

I'm also grateful to those who have helped me bring this project to fruition:

Simon Devenyi, for helping me organize and transfer my thoughts and original concept into a readable digital version.

Beth Parker, who organized the framework and helped me inject more lightness.

My two Kellys: Kelly McClymer, whose "Book Power Hours" and Kelly Falardeau, whose BAM program carried me over the line to get this book published and promoted.

Heidi Dunstan, whose confidence and skills smoothed some bumps.

Special thanks also to all the teachers and educators who tirelessly commit themselves to creating the best learning environment for our most precious geniuses: our children.

CONTENTS

READ THIS FIRST!

It was 1999 and I never expected to fall in love. Still reeling from the end of a 21-year relationship and marriage with my high school sweetheart, I was a single mom with 3 young children. Rather than returning to a career in taxation law after an extended maternity leave, I found myself sitting in a room in California with 35 seasoned educators. We were there to train as dyslexia correction facilitators. They were looking for a solution for their students. I was looking for a way to support my children in their education, and in particular, my "dangerously gifted" son who was extremely unhappy in school.

During many years as a classroom volunteer, I'd seen more than enough evidence that too many bright children were doing terribly in school. I saw families who struggled to complete daily homework. I also saw how gaps in the basic skills of reading and writing were crushing young students.

It was my turn to introduce myself to my fellow trainees. "My name is Diane Devenyi. I'm a former tax lawyer and mother of three and I'm here to revamp education on the planet." And then I sat down.

What did I just say? How does anyone do anything "on the planet"? (It was 1999, after all.) What could revamping education look like? I had no idea. I felt sure about one thing, however. I had found my calling: I was here to revamp education on the planet. And I was taking my first step.

My new colleagues and I soon learned how to facilitate a process for setting up a solid foundation for learning with focus and balance. It was simple and elegant and profound. Then I had an experience that I can recall to this day. I felt a connection that woke up every cell of my body, creating a bond that continues to grow, more than 20 years later. My life has never been the same as I share my love story everywhere I go. The object of my affection? The 26 letters of the English alphabet!

When using my hands, heart and imagination to re-learn the alphabet on that fateful day, everything changed. My entire body signalled a deep comprehension — and a feeling that my life was shifting. I was connecting to an aspect of my genius I never knew existed. Up until that day, I believed that learning was something that occurred only with our eyes, ears and brains. Learning the alphabet as a child by looking at it and singing The Alphabet Song, I found it easy to read and write. I never thought much about the symbols I had used every day for decades. Now my entire body was feeling them and I knew that I could never go back.

There was something about re-learning the letters in a holistic way that triggered my transformation. Today, my appreciation for and certainty of these symbols continue to give me unexplainable confidence to learn and try new things. Knowing how mastery of the alphabet feels, I seek that feeling with whatever I'm learning every day.

In the 20+ years since that experience, it's been my privilege to guide hundreds of children and adults as I have refined and expanded the alphabet learning process. Over time I've seen the power of solid learning and literacy foundations and marvelled at how each person finds their unique zone of genius through their hands, eyes and imagination.

Parents are thrilled to see a spark in their child's eyes that's been missing for years. A 77 year-old student woke up laughing every day, feeling smart for the first time in his life.

Whether adult or child, struggling or capable reader or writer, everyone can be enriched. The benefits flow to those who are learning English as their first language equally to those for whom English is a second or even fifth language. Successful foundations can be set for every type of learner who is starting their English journey. It's also possible at any time—even decades later—to fill in the gaps of an incomplete literacy education.

A joyful experience of learning is what I envision for every person in my quest to revamp education. And it all begins with the alphabet…and you!

YOU!

You are the amazing result of millions of years of evolution whose existence expands the universe.

Let's recap some highlights:

It's your birthday!

Your birth marked another miracle in the great web of life. You are pathetically helpless, but at the same time you have everything you need to grow and create a spectacular life. And just as an apple seed has the potential to become a majestic, fruit-bearing tree, you are encoded with gifts, talents and interests to make your unique mark in the world.

Your first step!

How many times did you try to walk and fall before that first step? It's a good thing that nobody gave up on you along the way. Everyone knew that it was only a matter of time before you would be independently mobile. And you are.

Your first word!

Let's be honest. It's not likely that your first sound was a full word, but that didn't stop you from making sounds and becoming the speaker you are today. You spent a lot of time watching and listening to the world around you before uttering your first word. Languages are complex. It takes time to learn them. And you did.

Your first day of school!

The day has arrived. It's time for you to go to school. The plan is for you to learn to read and write, plus do math and everything else you will need to become a valued member of society.

We know you are a marvel. You can walk, talk, run, feed and dress yourself, maybe catch a ball or sing. You were born to learn and grow. School is all about learning. It should be the best part of your day and set you up for lifelong success.

The School Experience

"I never read much in school.
I got really bad grades — D's and F's and C's
in some classes, and A's and B's in others.
In the second week of the 11th grade, I just quit.
When I was in school, it was really difficult.
Almost everything I learned,
I had to learn by listening.
My report cards always said that I was
not living up to my potential."

— Cher,
Actor and Singer

7

CHAPTER 1
YOU ARE NOT ALONE

One step forward, many steps back.

But when you could not read or write "at grade level," or do math the way you were taught, what happened? Did your teachers know how to help you resolve your confusion, reduce your stress, or improve focus? Or were you told that you were slower than others? Did you ever wish, but gave up hope, that you'd get an A?

I believe this means that you're smarter and more creative than you realize. It also means that you were misunderstood by the system. You're not alone.

The stories below are meant to inspire you. Each one is of a student I've known or worked with who came up against an obstacle, perhaps a mis-diagnosis, a language barrier, some kind of mis-understanding. My bet is that you'll recognize yourself in at least one of these stories.

Read on … which ones sound familiar to you?

So there I was in a special education class

Eight-year-old Blair was struggling with reading, writing and arithmetic. He had been in a special education class for two years because he seemed "slow." His printing was so bad that it was decided that he had a "fine motor skill" issue. He visited an occupational therapist every week for a year. After all of this "help," when he was asked to print out both an upper and a lower case alphabet, this is all he could write:

A B C D e F O G H I b K I n o P Q r S T U V W Y Z

Then Blair spent a day and a half relearning the alphabet. He was so proud and wanted to surprise his teacher. He wrote this note all by himself:

Dear Miss
I want to show
you how good I
can print now.
abcdefghijk lmnop qrstuvwx
yz

ABCDEFGHIJKLMN
OPQR ST UVWXYZ

Blair shocked a lot of people!

I was given a computer because I couldn't write properly

Everyone knew that eighteen-year-old Brent was really smart. He had taught himself to design and program video games.

He also had gruesome writing. It was so bad that he was permitted to use a laptop for everything. Teachers were not allowed to require him to write anything by hand.

The conclusion from everyone: Brent would never be able to write neatly. After a day and a half of learning the alphabet in a new way, however, his writing became neat and legible.

I just needed to believe I was smart and use the right approach

Thomas struggled with reading and had all but given up, but eventually he found his motivation to keep going. At 14, he knew he wanted his girlfriend to think he was smart. With a clear goal, Thomas unlocked barriers. By using an approach that matched his skills, his reading finally improved.

My first language wasn't English and I lacked focus

Out of all her students at the beginning of the school year, a certain caring and committed teacher was most worried about five-year-old Rhea. Rhea lacked focus and stared at the ceiling or out the windows during lessons. As a child of recent refugees, she didn't know the English alphabet. The teacher was not sure how to help her.

Our solution was to begin with "learning warm-ups" and improve her focus. We practised balance and played with balls. At first, Rhea had no clue how to catch a ball. I had to place the ball in her hand and show her how to close her fingers around it. Eventually, she learned to grasp a ball dropped into her outstretched hand. As we gradually increased the distance between us, a much-focused little girl could catch a ball from the same distance as her classmates.

Rhea grinned from ear to ear at her first successful catch. In my mind's eye I imagined that a graph showing her life's path for achieving her destiny had just skyrocketed.

Another thing skyrocketed: By the end of the school year, Rhea was one of the strongest readers in her class.

So what have we learned, class?

There are various reasons why the students in the above examples struggled. Blair and Brent were mis-diagnosed. Thomas needed first to believe that he was smart and that he was important in someone's life before he was ready to use a new approach that changed everything.

It's easier to learn when you're treated as though you matter. The connection that comes from being valued motivates us to try harder and achieve greater success. (How many teachers helped you to feel important? Hopefully there were a few.)

Even those amazing teachers out there who want more for their students — such as Rhea's kindergarten teacher — are caught in a system that isn't meeting diverse needs. Resolving Rhea's coordination issue was a critical first step in revealing her genius. Balance freed her brilliant brain to focus on learning and then excel in reading.

Too often, teachers are not trained to prepare every student to be ready to learn. And large classes also make it difficult for teachers to give each student the attention they need.

Stop doubting yourself!

THERE'S NOTHING WRONG WITH YOU!

How smart do you think you are? Was school a great part of your day or was it terrible? You may have been good at some things. You may have felt that you were good at nothing.

Did you spend more time paying attention to your weaknesses — rather than your strengths? Did you end up feeling a little inadequate about some things? If so, you're not alone.

The result: Just as with Blair, Brent, Thomas and Rhea, at some point one or all of these conclusions were made about you:
1. Laziness — you have to try harder
2. Low intelligence — you're not that smart
3. Fine motor skill problems — you are just uncoordinated

Perhaps you thought one or all of these things applied to you. Maybe your teachers told your parents these things about you. Maybe other kids (including your siblings) made fun of you.

You are enough!

The students in the above examples were able to overcome their challenges with a simple process. They first identified their own learning gaps and then used hands-on approaches that finally worked for them to fill in those gaps. And it's not too late for you to do the same. At any age, with the right mindset and methods, we can all be successful and literate lifelong learners.

It's time to put aside old stories and labels. It's time to learn the truth about who you really are. You were born to learn. Inside each one of you is a genius waiting to be revealed.

CHAPTER 2

THE MIS-UNDERSTOOD, MIS-DIAGNOSED AND THE SIMPLY "MISSED"

"Thousands of geniuses live and die undiscovered
— either by themselves or by others."
— Mark Twain,
American Writer, Humorist, Entrepreneur and Lecturer

There's another serious situation that many students encounter early in their education: The effect of the school experience? They end up feeling like failures.

Consider ten-year-old Oliver. An engaging, popular student, everyone was impressed by his breadth of knowledge and vocabulary. His mother was shocked therefore when he brought home a report card that said he was failing at writing. He couldn't put his brilliant thoughts into coherent written language. She knew that he struggled with spelling, but he was so confident, smart and articulate. He was reading books beyond his age. How could he be failing writing?

When she asked his teacher what she should do, she was even more shocked by the answer: "Be very worried," the teacher said.

Misunderstandings lead to many inaccurate conclusions about students who don't succeed with traditional literacy methods. It's understood that reading and writing are critical skills for successful learning. And most students appear to respond well to the current teaching methods.

Therefore, a student's failure to learn in a traditional way must mean there's something delayed, slow or otherwise wrong with the student. Or there's something wrong about how the parents are supporting their child's learning at home.

Not so fast. This simply is not true.

> It's very common for parents who express concern about their child's lack of reading skills to be told to spend more time reading to their child — even if they are already putting in the time!

Your teachers had a job they were never trained to do. Most wanted to help but didn't know how. Their own education failed to provide the necessary tools needed to help every student learn to read and write. They were never taught about a significant root cause of many learning and literacy issues.

Nor did they know that without the right approaches for you to skillfully read and write, you could grow up thinking there was something wrong with you — in short, that as a person, you were somehow lacking. You were "not enough."

Also, very few teachers are taught that issues relating to poor handwriting and spelling can lead to a range of physiological and psychological issues.

Did your teachers ever say to you, "Do you know that many smart and creative people have messy handwriting or poor spelling?" Probably not. Don't blame them, though. They didn't know and most still don't today.

The shocking, sad and scary facts about feeling "less" than expected

Do you know what can happen to smart and creative people who feel as if they're stupid, lazy or clumsy?

Combo packs of other issues show up. These can include:

- ADD/ADHD
- Frequent headaches
- Frequent stomach aches
- School avoidance and dropouts
- Low self-esteem
- Low confidence
- Stuttering
- Stress
- Skin issues
- Misbehaving
- Bullying — either as bully or victim
- Bed wetting

I've worked with many people who had one or more of these issues, and no one really knew why. Doctors and specialists couldn't provide solutions.

Take a moment and think about it. Were any of
the following statements made about you?

Some people are just slow at learning.
You must be one of those people.

Some people have a low IQ.
You must have a low IQ.

Some people are too uncoordinated
to print by hand.
You must have a "fine motor skill" issue.

Some people are terrible spellers.
You must be one of those people.

Sorry, you just don't have what it takes to learn
reading and writing skills.

You seem quite smart so you must be lazy.
Just try harder.

Apply yourself!

One six-year-old boy had headaches every day he went to school. When I started working with James, he was so nervous that his hands melted the modeling clay we were using. Happily, it wasn't long before he learned to read and write for the first time. And his headaches suddenly disappeared.

Eight-year-old Matthew struggled with literacy and was placed in a special education class. He also stuttered badly and sounded as though he had marbles in his mouth. Nobody could understand him. With the right approach to learning, he suddenly spoke beautifully. He was even invited to offer "words of wisdom" during every lunch to a crowded dining hall. No one would have believed that he ever had a speech issue.

Unfortunately, these issues don't always resolve themselves. It's rare for children to "grow out" of them. If left unresolved, they can continue to haunt people, even as adults.

At 45, Jane was a professional report writer. Reading and writing were never an issue for her. Math was, however. She barely passed high school math and avoided anything to do with numerals. After she relearned the alphabet and numerals in clay, using her hands and imagination, it all suddenly made sense. She even recalled and understood Pythagorean Theorem!

An unfortunate path to "learned helplessness"

Many well-meaning teachers believe that some students lack the ability to complete the requirements for a high school diploma. If their community has social support programs and financial assistance for adult disabilities, these students are directed to a future of reliance on such systems.

The idea that they cannot possibly become self-supporting is reinforced in meetings that are held once every year until the student is old enough to receive "assistance" money from the state.

One student told me that her entire "schooling" felt like one long babysitting session, where simple activities were used to pass the time. This is what many teachers have been trained to provide. What's worse is that these classes cost a lot of money because the student-teacher ratio is so low. Sadly, once placed in this stream, it's almost impossible to escape.

Teachers in these classes are given the job to occupy and keep these students cooperative until they can be passed on to the next level. Eventually, the adult community social net then takes the baton in the relay race to nowhere in particular.

For most people involved in this process, there's a point after which they feel there's no hope to turn things around. The students no longer believe in themselves and nor does anyone else. They learn to feel helpless and their lives play out as predicted by the teachers and social workers.

Thankfully, It doesn't have to be this way. It's time for the truth!

Congratulations, you can't read, write or spell!

I actually believe that it's a good thing when someone can't read, write or spell well, or that their handwriting is a mess. I find that they're usually smart and talented and will be more than capable of developing perseverance, self-appreciation and talents — both known and unknown.

I learned this by working with a lot of really creative and smart people who also thought they were stupid, or lazy, or both. School was not easy or fun for them and they couldn't wait to get out. Every one of them had one or more of these issues:

- Messy handwriting
- Poor spelling
- Slow to understand what they read
- Struggle to put ideas into written or spoken words
- Inconsistent focus

Like you, they were expected to do what they were taught, but couldn't. Their experiences made them feel that there was something wrong with them. They began to believe in words such as "stupid" and use phrases such as, "I suck at math." How is it that the place intended for learning is causing so much suffering and can lead to feelings of stupidity?

The power of self-worth

"In high school I was labeled the girl least likely to succeed.
I remember a teacher would say in front of the class:
'What are you, stupid?'"

— Erin Brockovich,
Legal Investigator, Environmental Activist

Marisa Peer is an author and inspirational speaker who has turned around thousands of lives with one message. Many of her clients are the super famous and super rich. Despite having everything, they lack a sense of self-worth. Marisa points out that scientists have shown that the harsh, hurtful, critical words we say to ourselves are a major cause of depression.

She teaches how authentic self-praise is more powerful than praise we receive from others. And that if we heard one simple statement every day until it became our internal belief, a major shift could occur in the world. The statement?

I am enough!

Pause here before you go on to the next chapter

What does "I am enough" mean? Say these words out loud to yourself:

- I matter.

- I deserve love, happiness and abundance.

- I have everything I need to create a spectacular life

- My challenges are perfectly designed to develop my unique gifts.

- The world is greater because I'm in it.

As you read this book, remind yourself of these statements. Realize that you are not broken. You are perfect. You are enough. Enough said.

Now let's get on with solving the problem.

It's Time To Find Out What Is Really Going On Here!

"I had lots of trouble in school as a child, and
I lost confidence. Teachers thought I was stupid.
I learned to read very late, when I was 11.
Dyslexia wasn't recognized then and the assumption
was you were incapable of thinking."

— Richard Rogers,
Architect

CHAPTER 3

YOUR LETTER DIS-ORDER IS SHOWING

If you have reading, writing or attention problems, you are not stupid, lazy or clumsy. Let's take that thorn out of your paw. You're just showing letter dis-order.

Yup, LETTER DIS-ORDER.

How do you feel about the phrase "letter dis-order?" Does it make you feel that there's something wrong with you?

So excuse me while I beg, but it's so important that you get this message: Please, please, please, believe me when I tell you that letter dis-order is not a diagnosis of a flaw in the person. It is simply something that can be assessed to find a hidden root cause of reading, writing or spelling issues.

Letter dis-order may sound serious but it's not.

Letter dis-order simply shows that your alphabet foundation is incomplete— for now.

Alphabet certainty is important because you can't read or write well without it. It may seem simple, but each letter has specific rules about how it looks and where it belongs relative to the other letters. Without certainty about these rules, letter dis-order can have a big impact on your life in many ways. So, why then have you never heard about it?

Actually, very few people have heard about letter dis-order. During my research into reading and writing problems, I saw the signs and impact of this fundamental issue and needed to come up with a suitable name for it; a name that could describe the effect of gaps in alphabet certainty. Armed with a name, I could then assess what was going on, and offer a way to resolve the problems.

Getting things in order

To understand dis-order, we must first appreciate its opposite: order, and the idea of convention.

There are three tests to indicate that a thing is in order. All parts involved must be in their conventional place, position and condition. You may be wondering, what does "conventional" mean?

"Conventional" things follow a community's "convention" about them. We're not talking here about a gathering of people — perhaps all wearing name tags and listening to some keynote speaker dispense wisdom from a podium. Rather, conventions around customs, rules or practices that are established by usage.

Think of the way religious conventions guide celebrations, funerals and daily routines; how sports conventions dictate game play, plus who wins; or the conventions we see every day that keep our lives in order.

Conventions such as setting a table when we eat meals, or how we greet people, make our lives more predictable, safer and easier. When we learn to use a convention, we have more time to play with our thoughts and words — or just play. Imagine trying to agree on new rules of play every time a professional team played a sport. It would be no fun for anyone!

Now let's get back to "order."

Remember that for anything to be in "order" there are three tests: place, position and condition.

A conventional place setting at a table (in the western world), for example, has tests for place and position with respect to the cutlery and dishes used — plus a specific condition.

Place: The plate is in the centre. The forks are placed to the left of the plate. The smaller fork is left of the large fork. The larger fork is between the small fork and the plate. The knife is to the right of the plate. The spoon is to the right of the knife.

Position: There is also a conventional position for each piece of the setting. The handles of the cutlery are pointing down, closer to the person who uses them. The cutlery is easy to pick up this way. They are also face-up, ready to be used, just like the plate.

Condition: Can you guess one conventional condition for the items in a place setting? (Hint: Do you like to eat from a dirty plate?) Yes, you want the items to be clean! Can you think of another conventional condition for plates and cutlery? If you guessed that they should be whole — not chipped or broken — and straight, not bent or twisted, then you're right.

As you can see, even with something as simple as a place-setting, there are many details that must be satisfied to have things in order.

Finding things in dis-order

In contrast to order, dis-order occurs when there is at least one thing that is not in its conventional place, position or condition. Any single missing element is enough. While there are three components to create order, only one of those missing components causes dis-order. Of course, if there are two, three or more things that are not in order, that's also dis-order.

Here's an example of three types of dis-order. Can you spot them?

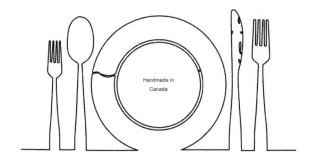

Answer:

The spoon and fork are in each other's place.

The plate is upside-down.

The knife is dirty.

Your clothes closet can provide another example of order versus dis-order. Your clothes are in order when they are in their conventional:

Place:
Clothes go in the closet, not on your bed, a chair or the floor.

Position:
Clothes hang neatly on hangers or lie folded in drawers or on shelves.

Condition:
Clothes are clean and smooth, not wrinkled. No holes.

Hmm, maybe there's some disorder there. That's okay. Let's return to literacy.

What if we got rid of those question marks, periods, nouns and verbs?

Literary conventions assist clear communication. All of those letters, punctuation marks, spelling and grammar rules exist so that everyone can be on the same page.

The conventions also free up our brains to explore and be creative while we write. Who wants to think about whether our writing is understandable when we'd rather build an epic story or compose the sweetest love letter ever?

There's a saying out there:
"With structure comes freedom."
It's worth paying attention to.

Time to push back a bit

Feeling a bit rebellious? Perhaps you want to break a few rules, push back against convention? I can relate, believe me! You have to choose your battles, however. Decide when following a convention is going to benefit you (such as writing down clear instructions when someone's minding your dog because Marley needs his meds) and when you can throw a "convention switch" to express your own creativity (leaving out a choice of treats).

> "I think people are afraid to add more structure to their day because it seems rigid or confining but the thing is, the more success you have, the more responsibility you'll have. Then the challenge becomes how to balance it all. The best way to balance is by creating routines to keep productive momentum going."
> — Wade Alters,
> Life Coach

Back to letter order

Now that you understand "order versus dis-order" and the benefit of writing conventions, what are the conventional places, positions and conditions for the letters of the alphabet? It's actually pretty simple when you know what you're looking for.

With respect to letters being in order, we may be thinking about "alphabetical order," or sequence, as follows:
A B C D E F G H I J K L M N O P Q R S T U V W X Y Z

"Order" in this sense refers to "the way things follow each other, one after another." As with a place setting, however, letter dis-order can occur in many ways, and affect placement, position or condition. And it only takes one type of dis-order of just one letter to cause letter dis-order in writing.

Let's see how the triple test for "order" applies to letters and to words.

Letter dis-order of placement

If you're asked to print out the upper case alphabet (capital letters) and mix in some lower case (small) letters, or mix up the order of the letters, then you're showing dis-order of placement. A common form of letter dis-order of placement is the misspelling of words. When you mix up the correct spelling of a word, it's dis-order because the letters are not in their conventional place.

Here are real-life examples that I've seen:

Placement dis-order of the alphabet
(mixed up sequence and case)

Print the UPPER CASE alphabet from A to Z

A B C d e f g h i j k l m N o p q K S t u v W x

Placement dis-order of words (misspelled)

I like Tarea Becus it is rell fun.
It is cool becus it has awsome stufe.
It is so fun. I love it so much.
I have 2 frends and thay like Tarana
to. We have a grop callba tarana.

Letter dis-order also occurs when letters are not in their conventional position. "Position" dis-order happens when the spacing between the letters is inconsistent or the location of a letter on the line is not accurate. There is also position disorder when letters are reversed. The conventional position for the lower case English alphabet is as follows:

a b c d e f g h i j k l m n o p q r s t u v w x y z

As you can see, every letter is in contact with the line, but some letters are written both above and below the line. Check out some examples below:

Spacing dis-order:

abcde f g hij k l m n o p q r s y z

Incorrect position on the line:

a, b, c, d, e, f, g, h, i, j, k, l, m, n, o, p, q, r, s
t, u, v, w, x, y, z

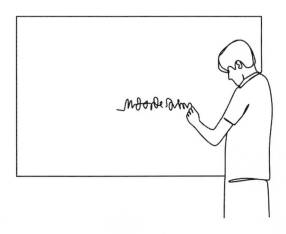

Letter dis-order of condition

In the third test for letter dis-order, we consider each letter's conventional condition. This type of letter dis-order is the one most people call "messy handwriting." There are two ways for letters to have an non-conventional condition:

1. Letters are poorly formed.
2. Letters are the wrong size, either too small or large when compared with the other letters.

Note about letter sizes:

For upper case letters, size is simple: every letter sits above the line and is the same height as the others.

Lower case letters have various size requirements. Some are approximately half the size of upper case letters (depending on the font) such as a, c, e, i, m, n, o, r, s, u, v, w, x, z. Some are the same size as upper case letters and sit entirely above the line (b, d, f, h, k, l, t). Some are the same size as upper case letters but sit both below and above the line (g, j, p, q, y).

Unless you had someone make sure you were certain about these differences, you may find these rules confusing. The example below shows profound confusion.

Letter dis-order for condition (and other issues):

Print the UPPER CASE alphabet from A to Z.

ARC DE F GHIJK LM opqRSTU VWXY
Z

Print the lower case alphabet from a to z.

abcbepahjdklMNopqrstuvwxyz

And now, for your brain's side of the story

Let's get to the heart of the matter.

If you're not sure about how to write out every letter, or wonder where each letter belongs on the line, then your alphabet learning is incomplete. In fact, that's why you show letter dis-order.

Here's why many people believe it happens: Your powerful brain has recorded every version of each letter you have ever seen in your life. Millions of images are floating around in your imagination. And your brain is ready to access them every time you read or write.

How awesome is that? Because you have a vivid imagination, however, it gets complicated.

One problem is that your brain hasn't been trained yet to see what's objectively in front of you when you read and write. You may look at words on a page and see letters that are not even there — or they may be moving around! You have a great imagination but it's out of control.

Add to this the fact that you haven't learned yet to choose and consistently use one standard version of each letter as you read and write. A "standard" is what you compare against other versions of the same item so that you can recognise it in a way that makes sense to you. Like conventions, standards make life easier.

Consider that today, we read many font styles, and some letters really vary from font to font. For example, consider a and a, or g and g. And there are lots more!

Without a standard reference letter, every possible version of each letter stays available to you and your brain keeps reviewing them all. It has no default of a consistent standard for each letter. Because your brain wants to resolve your doubts or questions, it's always working in the background. It's trying to figure out the stuff you're not sure about. Talk about a distraction!

This isn't because you lack the ability to choose the best version of each letter, but because no one taught you how to make your personal standard version of each letter. You don't have a clear and consistent image in your mind of how each letter should look. And your creative imagination is not helping.

The result? You get confused by all of the potential choices.

If your teachers never personally experienced this type of confusion themselves — and may not have known that it exists for other people because nobody taught them about it — then they couldn't help you resolve it. Even if they were trained in a fantastic evidence-based reading program.

Your results in any reading or writing program will be limited until you resolve your confusion. And you will struggle when you don't need to.

Alphabet confusion can lead to gaps that may show up in your handwriting. They may mess up your spelling, your reading, or your ability to put your thoughts into words.

If you find reading and writing difficult, then all subjects are affected — even math (think "word problems"). Gaps in alphabet foundation make your brain work harder. First they distract; then they interfere with learning other things. These gaps cause a lot of problems and can get in the way of the fullest expression of your natural genius.

And school goes downhill from there. So does learning!

To all the athletes, artists, actors, scientists, musicians and other creative types

Are you wondering why I call you "Genius?"

It's because each of us has special skills that support and help us to develop our talents. You may not even know you have these skills — and you may be using them all the time.

These skills could include the ability to imagine pictures, visualize goals, become a character, or see inventions. You could say that you are "bending reality" and seeing things that your physical eyes cannot see. You are instead seeing with your "mind's eye" — also known as your imagination.

Did you know that professional athletes have been known to see the stitching on a baseball as it approaches the plate at 100 miles (160 kilometers) per hour? That's bending reality!

Here are some interesting questions about creativity:

How did Picasso or Modigliani see their subjects? Did they view them as mixed up or elongated portraits? Or do we enjoy the imagination and goals that they artfully expressed on canvas?

How do actors become someone else in front of our very eyes? How do directors know how to direct? Where do the stories in a writer's imagination come from?

How did Einstein imagine a theory of relativity for astronomers to eventually prove?

To bend reality requires that you "remove" yourself from the traditional or "objective" orientation of your five senses.

Have you ever been in a stopped car at a traffic light and felt that you were rolling backward as the car beside you moved forward?

That's disorientation. You experienced an unseen, unheard or unfelt reality.

You weren't moving, but you sure felt that you were!

At other times and in other ways — you may use disorientations to create objects or experiences for yourself and others, as an artist, athlete or scientist.

With great power comes great responsibility

There can be a problem with disorientation, however, when you want to read or write. You may be used to using your mind's eye away from your body for unique ways of bending reality. Or of having visions or pictures that float around in your imagination. But for reading or writing you are looking at words on a page or a screen in front of you. Do you see (pun intended) how things can get mixed up without a plan?

The good news is that you can "warm up" your eyes, your brain and your body to set them up, or "orient" them, for accurate reading and writing. Eliminate disorientation and confusion. Feel good as you focus. No more stress or headaches.

The even better news is that you can choose when and how to orient and disorient yourself. Use your mind's eye one way for reading and writing, and in other ways for sports, dance, creating and performing.

The best news of all is that your imagination for learning is already great — even if you didn't know it. And you can learn to use it to succeed in everything else you do!

"My imagination, which I think is the gift of dyslexia,
is what's also given me
different kinds of insights into character, and also
into the way that I live my life."

— Orlando Bloom,
Actor

CHAPTER 4

THE POWER BEHIND THOSE ABC'S

"Let's start at the very beginning, a very good place to start.
When you read you begin with A, B, C..."

— "Doe a Deer" from *The Sound of Music*

Maria — the governess in the *The Sound of Music* — took it for granted that learning to read begins with the alphabet. She was right. What I've learned, however, is that it's not enough to simply recite the letters. The best foundation starts with absolute certainty of every letter.

Alphabet certainty includes knowing the letters in perfect sequence, forward and backward. Being able to print every letter accurately is also a part of the process. And making the entire alphabet out of clay is a powerful tool for learning the alphabet. This connects learning between your hands and your brain.

You may be thinking, "What do you mean I don't know the alphabet? Of course I know the alphabet. After all, I can sing *The Alphabet Song*. I know what each letter is called."

Sorry, but knowing the words to a rhyming song is NOT alphabet certainty. It may be certainty of lyrics and a melody, but it is not a deep knowing of the symbols of the alphabet.

The Alphabet Song is actually a crutch that misleads people into believing that the alphabet is being learned. (Here's a quick test for you: If you have to sing *The Alphabet Song* to yourself to figure out which letters come after "k" or "r" right now, then you have work to do ;-)

Is letter dis-order caused by letter confusion?

You may have been wondering at some point whether letter dis-order is simply caused by confusion. Yes! It is. And that's all it is: unresolved confusion, or uncertainty, about one or more letters.

(I could have focused on "letter confusion" in this book but I believe the term "letter dis-order" is a more accurate phrase that leads to a deeper understanding of the issue … and its objective solution.)

Your teachers may not have known about letter certainty, by the way. They were taught to teach you about the alphabet by showing you what the letters look like on paper. They may have given you sandpaper letters to help you learn through touching them.

But they never heard about having proper orientation first and then using your hands to gain alphabet certainty.

Plus, teachers feel constant pressure to cover the entire curriculum. If they see that the teaching method doesn't work for you, they still need you to please hurry along and learn the lesson. Stress (for everyone) plus confusion is a perfect recipe for letter dis-order.

The emotional and scary truth about letter confusion

Because letter dis-order demonstrates unresolved confusion about the alphabet, over time any discomfort you feel about your confusion may connect with stronger negative emotions.

As your confusion continues to exist, your gaps affect not only reading and writing, they can begin to grow emotional connections in your brain between confusion, reading, writing and learning in general.

Every time you're unable to read, write or spell a word, it develops another "confusion" connection in your brain. At some point confusion becomes attached to fear: fear that you'll never get it; fear that your brain must be broken; fear that you're different from everyone else and fear that you'll be rejected.

Humans evolved to fear separation because it's safer and easier to survive in groups. We create shelter, find food and avoid predators better when we're together. We are wired to seek companionship. But you feel different and are now worried that you don't fit in!

These negative connections between learning, isolation, fear and confusion continue to affect your brain's ability to focus, build positive connections and learn many things. You begin to doubt your ability or intelligence. This can result in new connections between confusion and doubt, confusion and weakness and confusion and low expectations. Over time we reinforce these connections, again and again. Eventually they become our dominant beliefs. Luckily, beliefs can change.

A word in favour of "good" confusion

It's time to get clear about confusion. Confusion is a natural companion to learning. When something is new, our brain has to find a way to fit it into our picture of the world. Until new patterns are created, we live with temporary confusion. If the confusion remains unresolved over time, it can create gaps like missing puzzle pieces in our overall picture.

People who are comfortable with temporary confusion and learning gaps find it easier to learn new things. Their emotions support learning. They know that the learning process takes as long as it takes. It's simply a matter of taking one step at a time until their brain finds the missing pieces.

Confusion eventually gives way to new knowledge — sometimes quickly, sometimes slowly.

This positive attitude toward learning is called a "growth mindset." It leads to greater success in learning. The best news about growth mindset is that anyone can develop it with the right environment and experiences.

But what happens when the pieces never fit?

Shift can happen, so shift your beliefs

I hope that by now you realize that reading, writing, focus and spelling challenges simply reveal an incomplete literacy education. And once the alphabet is truly learned, the door opens to a whole new world of reading for pleasure, writing neatly, spelling accurately and writing down your brilliant thoughts with ease.

Your job now is to begin to believe in yourself and know that you are born to learn and that certainty takes time. If confusion makes you fear learning, it's never too late to shift your beliefs. You'll soon accept — and then embrace — the fact that your confusion is a sign that you're learning something new.

Or, is this you?

Your letter dis-order may not seem like a big deal after all these years. You are over the embarrassment of messy handwriting or poor spelling, and successful in other ways. I hear you. But don't you want to give your brain a boost and feel even a little bit smarter about this irritation? What about no longer being distracted every day by something that you can resolve in a matter of hours?

The best way to remove unhelpful connections is to replace them with new, empowering ones. I've seen that relearning the alphabet can create positive new introductions between confusion and learning success, confusion and belonging, and confusion and joy. Practice then makes progress and it's not long before a growth mindset emerges. Confusion becomes a welcome companion to lifelong learning.

This approach to learning begins with a supportive, inclusive learning community. There's a demonstrated commitment to success for all that offers you freedom from the fear of separation. Your unique ways are celebrated and you see for yourself what I've known about you all along: how well-designed you are to create a life of meaningful contribution and joy.

Removing The Darkness

"I was dyslexic before anybody knew what dyslexia was.
I was called 'slow.' It's an awful feeling to think
of yourself as 'slow' — it's horrible."

— Robert Benton,
Film Writer and Director

CHAPTER 5

TIME FOR SOME MYTH BUSTING!

Now you know … and there's no going back. Letter dis-order has nothing to do with laziness or stupidity.

Let's recap: Letter dis-order starts as natural confusion that occurs while learning anything new. If your alphabet learning is incomplete, it's likely that you have unresolved confusion about one or more letters. That confusion affects your ability to learn other subjects or skills. As the story repeats itself, at some point the conclusion is made that there's something wrong with your brain, your attitude — or both.

So let's look at the various ways your "dis-order" may be showing and then do some serious myth busting about why these issues don't mean that you're lazy, or stupid, or need to try harder to fix your motor skills!

- Messy handwriting (cursive and/or printed)
- Poor spelling
- Low reading levels
- Inconsistent attention and focus
- Difficulty putting thoughts into written or spoken words
- Behaviour or motivation problems

Myth Busting: Messy writing

Myth 1: Messy writing is caused by low intelligence.

Have you noticed how many times I've said that your messy writing means that you're smart and creative? It's true. Think about it. The classic messy writers — doctors — are no mental slouches, right? Neither are you.

> "You may not be able to read a doctor's handwriting
> and prescription, but you'll notice
> [the] bills are neatly typewritten."
>
> — Earl Wilson,
> Journalist

And let's not forget Brent. At 18, there was no doubt that he was brilliant but he could not print legibly. After all those years of frustration, a simple hands-on approach for relearning the letters opened him up to new choices that no one believed were possible. For the first time in his life he could choose whether he wanted to print legibly. Imagine the feeling of having that freedom overnight!

Myth 2: Messy handwriting is caused by fine motor skill issues.

When many people with messy handwriting are asked to make a drawing, their drawing skills are usually fine — sometimes great. They may not be Leonardo da Vinci (although some drawings are really good!) but it's easy to tell what their drawing represents. They can draw straight and curved lines. Question: If their fine motor skills work well for drawing, how could they be broken for writing?

The same applies to those skilled surgeons with messy handwriting. If they can perform surgery, they must have excellent fine motor skills. Something else must be causing their messy handwriting.

Also remember Blair, whose handwriting improved in under two days? He quickly turned around his unfixable "fine motor skill issues" because he finally used an approach that worked for him. He was so excited that he secretly wrote a note for his teacher.

Many students I have worked with who seemed to suddenly "fix" their motor skill issues have reported feeling a huge weight lifting from them—a weight they didn't realize they were carrying. I recall one student laughing as he printed his first legible words of his life. He could not believe they were coming from his hand!

Here's an example of letter dis-order when the drawing shows that fine motor skills are not an issue:

Print the UPPER CASE alphabet from A to Z.

A B C D e F J H I j K l M M o P Q R S Y Z

Print the lower case alphabet from a to z.

a b c d e f y h i j k l m n o p q r s y z

Myth 3: Messy handwriting comes from laziness.

Recently I worked with a nine-year-old boy who had messy handwriting. Both Anthony and his mother said the problem was that he was "just lazy." When I asked him to do his best to print out the alphabet for me, Anthony tried really hard and this was the best he could do:

After one and a half days of re-learning the alphabet, he could do this:

When his mother came to pick him up at the end of the workshop, Anthony was so excited that he ran back to the table to make a new drawing, caption and complete alphabet for his mother. This was not the behaviour of a lazy boy.

Anthony's messy writing had nothing to do with laziness, but his "laziness" may have been a response of hopelessness. He gave up hope after years of trying to write neatly and failing.

When Anthony transformed his letter dis-order into certainty, many things changed. New inspiration arose because his effort was producing results. His mother was thrilled with his beautiful, perfect spelling tests.

What qualifies as "messy writing?"

When I began writing this book I was focusing on what most people think is classic messy handwriting: mis-formed letters that are hard to read. Recently, however, I was contacted by a mother who was concerned about her twelve-year-old son's "messy writing." She told me that not one of Harry's teachers agreed that his writing was a problem. She decided to look outside the school system and found our workshops.

As he was completing a pre-workshop alphabet assessment, I peeked over his shoulder and saw this:

My first thoughts were, "OMG! That looks great. Harry's mother must be very demanding. I can imagine what his teachers thought when she complained about his hand-writing."

My opinion shifted, however, as his lower case letters appeared on the page:

Print the lower case alphabet from a to z.
abcdefghijklmnopqrstuvwxyz

Yes, the letters are neat, but they are not accurate. Check out the upper case alphabet. It looks good but there's something wrong. Can you tell what it is? (Hint: there's a letter missing.) Also, how many lower case letters have size or placement issues?

Harry's mother's intuition about her son's handwriting was correct. She knew that something wasn't right. She felt that until he fixed whatever his problem was, it would be difficult for him to reach his fullest potential academically.

This experience helped me see that I needed to expand my focus on "messy writing" to include any printing or writing where there's inaccuracy, that is, where there's dis-order. That's how I came up with the phrase "letter dis-order."

Over the years I have seen many examples of neat, legible writing that hides the gaps that can interfere with a person's focus, learning and literacy success. That's why I recommend that everyone starts with the simple assessment to identify lack or order—or dis-order—in their alphabet.

The next chapter has more examples of assessments, plus a description of how to do these assessments in chapter 6.

Myth Busting: Poor spelling

Do you ever wonder what people think about you when you mis-spell words?

Do you worry that they think you're stupid or lazy? How is it that you can read and understand the same words you can't spell on your own? Careful — your letter dis-order is showing again!

Until you resolve your confusion about the letters, the picture in your mind for both letters and words is still unclear. This lack of clarity frequently shows up as poor spelling.

They may not even realize it, but many good spellers can see words they're spelling in their imagination, or mind's eye. Like messy handwriting, you know that poor spelling is not caused by low intelligence or laziness. Right?

> "Writing and spelling were always terribly difficult for me. My letters were without originality.
> I was ... an extraordinarily bad speller and have remained so."
>
> — Agatha Christie,
> Mystery Writer and Novelist

Fortunately, it's possible to learn to spell better when you relearn the letters and eliminate letter dis-order. Good news: English spelling can be mastered, just as the letters can. Great news: It's never too late to start.

One eight-year-old boy was driving his teacher crazy. Trevor was bright, loved to read and was very helpful in class, but he couldn't do one thing: he was never able to accurately copy the weekly spelling list from the board into his notebook. He always had at least one word mis-spelled. And the word was right in front of him!

Both his teacher and parents thought that if he would just pay more attention and try harder, he would get every word right. But Trevor insisted that he was trying hard, and couldn't do it. Frustration!

How long would it take before he would give up trying entirely? (It's been my experience that the common age for hitting the wall and giving up is age ten or eleven.)

Fortunately, things turned around when Trevor became an alphabet "expert." His letter dis-order had been showing up as spelling mistakes. With his new confidence and certainty he was able to accurately copy the words and ace spelling tests. Phew!

Spelling challenges with English as a second language

For people learning English as a second or foreign language (ESL, EFL), it's common to have spelling issues. Not surprising because English is a crazy language to spell.

It becomes more complicated, however, when teachers don't understand why spelling problems are not being resolved over time. Why does the student need extra help learning English? Do they simply need more time with English, or are they a "slow learner" for learning languages generally?

A lack of awareness about letter dis-order can explain why many students are in special education classes as they learn English as a second language. The best approach for ESL or EFL classes is to have every student achieve alphabet certainty before learning spelling.

For some, the potential for good spelling will transform into great spelling. For others, it could be the difference between a lifetime of poor spelling versus spelling prowess. The best part is that the process that leads to proficiency with letters can naturally extend to success with spelling.

Get solid with the alphabet first. Then you avoid letter dis-order and any misunderstanding about capacity to learn English.

EE/E (e) EYE/EE (i) JEE/ZHAY (g) JAY/ZHEE (j)

Learning a new alphabet can be a challenge, especially if your first alphabet is completely different. But what if you are learning a new language that uses the same alphabet as your first language? Surprisingly, it can be equally — and sometimes more — confusing.

When I was working in a classroom of Anglophone students (English being their first language) who were in a French Immersion program (they study only French until third grade) the confusion ran wild. Why?

See the title of this section? It shows the pronunciation in English/French for the letters "e," "i," "g" and "j." The sounds reverse and overlap in ways that can be very confusing to students learning both languages. How can you keep things clear in your mind when the sound "ee" is the name for "e" in English and "i" in French, and that's just the beginning?

You know what I'm going to say: Enrich learning by using techniques to gain certainty of both alphabets first and prevent avoidable confusion.

Spelling and "fa-netiks." What??

It's true that English spelling is challenging, but it's not im-possible to learn to be a great speller. Many problems begin with the way English spelling is taught. Rather than teach the alphabet for certainty and then approach spelling, most teachers skip the essential alphabet foundation and move directly to spelling.

Another problem arises if there's a heavy emphasis on the use of "phonics" for learning how to pronounce and spell words. With phonics you focus on the sounds that letters represent. For example, the sounds of the letters "b," "a" and "t" combine to make the sound of the word "bat."

This approach has a place but is not sufficient with one of the most confusing languages on the planet to spell: English. One reason: The English language uses 44 different sounds (which are called "phonemes") but only 26 letters.

You're smart. Can you see the problem? It's impossible to make 44 sounds with 26 letters if each letter represents only one sound. Some letters must therefore represent more than one sound. You have to know which letters can do that. And then you have to learn about combinations of letters, which can also have more than one sound.

It goes on and on. As a combination of many languages, English uses inconsistent spellings. The result? Some words sound the same but look different (e.g., bear and bare). Others look the same but are pronounced differently (e.g. live, as in not pre-recorded, which rhymes with "hive" — and live, as in being alive, which rhymes with "give"). These lists go on and on. There are also some spellings that just make no logical sense (for example: "enough," "one" and "ptero- dactyl").

There are, in fact, so many ways to make some sounds that it can drive your logical mind crazy.

Here's my favourite example: "ough" can represent eight different sounds in English:

- "oo" as used in through (sounds like "true")
- "off" as used in cough
- "uff" as used in tough
- "aw" as used in thought
- "ow" as used in plough (sounds like "cow")
- "oh" as used in though
- "up" as used in hiccough and
- "och" as used in lough (sounds like "lock")

The result of all these variations is that a phonics-based approach only works for half the words in English. You have to master the rest to be a good speller. It has nothing to do with how smart you are. If nobody has taught you how to learn to properly spell in English, then it's time for you to get the job done yourself — now!

Know the alphabet with certainty first. Then study spelling.

What about just learning the rules in a better way? Sorry, if letter dis-order is a part of your reality, you need to know the alphabet with certainty before learning to spell. English words are almost impossible to spell when you're confused about the letters. It's that simple.

> "My spelling makes people laugh.
> It makes me laugh, actually."
>
> — Keira Knightley,
> Actor

I once trained two amazing special education teachers to assess and resolve letter dis-order with their students. Even though they had more than 50 years of teaching experience between them, they didn't know what to do with students who struggled with certain literacy issues. They were also really excited to support their students in new, effective ways.

As their training was ending, one of the teachers said, "This is great! On Monday, Wednesday and Friday, we'll learn alphabet foundation and on Tuesday and Thursday I'll teach spelling." Her colleague and I looked at each other, then at her. "Oops!" she exclaimed. "I almost did it again. I promise never to put curriculum before foundation ever again."

Myth Busting: Low reading levels

If you have never been a good reader, if you read slowly, or can't understand what you read, then your letter dis-order is showing up in this way. It makes sense. If you don't know the individual letters, then groups of letters are going to be a problem in some way. For you, it's with reading comprehension.

People (including teachers) make a lot of assumptions about intelligence when you can't read well. They may think that you're not smart.

I believe that we have it backward: it's hard to show how smart you are when reading is a problem. And until you learn the alphabet with certainty, reading will be an issue. It's ridiculous to make any conclusions about your intelligence in that case. All we know for certain is that you don't have a solid alphabet yet, and (no surprise here), you have a reading problem.

Myth Busting: Attention and focus

Seven-year-old Nathan was very distracted. He couldn't stay in his seat and wandered around disturbing other students. He visited the principal's office every day. Nothing could keep his attention for long — until he relearned the alphabet using his hands and his imagination. His focus and ability to sit still for a long time shocked his mother, his teacher and his principal.

Your brain wants to resolve the letter choice issue, but you don't have the tools to be focused and choose the right one. Instead, your brain is scanning hundreds or thousands of letters to unsuccessfully resolve your confusion.

Like Nathan, until you've mastered the alphabet, your brain will have unnecessary distraction. This distraction effect happens whether you're reading, writing by hand, or keying in words on an electronic device (why?), because each of those activities requires interaction with letters.

Some people manage confusion and mind chatter well. Others sink deeper into confusion and more distraction until reading, writing and spelling feel nearly impossible.

Scientists have proven that distractions can cause forgetfulness, inconsistent focus (ADHD) and reduced capacity in the workplace (meaning that you waste a lot of time). With letter dis-order distractions, it's a miracle that you get anything done at all. You must have superpowers!

As you build your personal alphabet certainty you not only resolve letter dis-order and its distractions, you also show your brain and body how to feel clarity in any new activity you choose. Bonus! Your ability to learn new things is improved because you've learned a method to resolve confusion and focus accurately as you learn any skill.

Myth Busting: Trouble putting thoughts into writing

Many smart people can read well but can't put their thoughts into written words. They are also likely to spell poorly.

How are you supposed to write your best without a solid alphabet as your guide? You can't.

In my experience, people with reading or writing issues are curious, deep thinkers, sensitive and creative. If literacy is challenging for you, that's probably true for you, too.

Right now you have unlimited versions of each letter running over and over again in your imagination. Without a process for choosing the right letters and words with certainty. This causes a distraction (as we talked about above) that makes reading or writing harder than it needs to be for you.

The solution? Connect your accurately-oriented mind's eye and body to create and confirm your standard version of each letter.

With a standard version for each letter, your connection to the letters shifts and you no longer have distracting thoughts about them as you read. Whether the thoughts are conscious or subconscious is less important than the fact that they can be resolved — by you.

The next step is to extend your letter certainty by improving your spelling first and then increasing your brain's ability to connect written words to their meanings.

You will also unlock access to written language as you feel differently about it. Imagine what can happen when you relate to the alphabet with certainty, resolve your confusion and become more able to write the amazing thoughts going on in your head.

Old distractions fall away, allowing you to be who you really are: a genius with brilliant ideas.

Myth Busting: Gifted LD

What about "giftedness" (usually a label given to those with an IQ in the top 2% of the population)?

Schools that assess children for "giftedness," frequently mis-assess those who show letter dis-order.

Remember Trevor, the boy with spelling issues? When tested for "giftedness" in school-wide testing with a written test, they said he did not qualify for the standard of being above the 98th percentile in IQ. But when privately tested with oral and written tests, some of his abilities were off the charts. His overall IQ was assessed at being above the 99th percentile (less than 1% of the population scores higher).

One way to more accurately assess giftedness and potential gaps is to give tests both in written and oral form. There are many students who score significantly higher for IQ when tested orally than by a written test alone.

(By the way, when the psychologist asked Trevor to guess his IQ percentile before giving him the test results, Trevor predicted that he was only at the 75th percentile. It is sad to think of how many people fail to know and enjoy their own true genius.)

Those students who test at or above the 98th percentile and also struggle with literacy issues may be given a label such as "Gifted Learning Disabled" or "Gifted LD." Maybe you were one of those students.

Just as with all literacy issues, any challenges among "gifted" students can be easily assessed and are often resolved when underlying letter dis-order is corrected. These students also demonstrate that many very smart people have literacy gaps, and assumptions about the intelligence of any person with issues from gaps may be inaccurate.

Whether or not you were considered "gifted" you belong to a significant part of the population who are showing everyone that our school models have room for improvement. What's awesome is that the solution for you enriches everyone!

Myth Busting: Behaviour issues

At twelve years-old, Steven had been in a class for the "mildly intellectually delayed" for several years. He often spoke out in class and was quite intense. He struggled with math and could not read or write. Upon successfully relearning the alphabet he told his class that at first he never believed he could learn the alphabet forward and backward, but proudly declared, "Look at me now!" The next week, with twinkling eyes and a big grin, he reported that he had challenged his principal to recite the alphabet backward—and she couldn't.

Little steps lead to big changes.

Steven's entire demeanour shifted when he was finally successful at learning something that felt significant. This opened him up to seeing himself as a smart person for the first time in his life, as someone who could graduate from high school. Because he saw that he *could* learn to read, he replaced disruptive behaviour with strategies for learning success to earn attention—and praise for the first time in his life. He also enjoyed helping those who were still resolving their letter dis-order.

What's it like to be expected to learn something without having the right tools to complete a lesson? You may know the feeling well but those without the experience can only imagine how frustrating it would be. How can educators therefore see that it can lead to poor behaviour?

When I've had the chance to address teachers and teacher candidates (in teacher's college) about literacy issues, I immerse them in the feeling of confusion that their students know well. This may sound strange, but my presentation was based on my personal experience of taking the position of Secretary for the Ontario Bar Association Tax Section while I was in law school.

You see, even though I hadn't taken a course in taxation law yet, I thought I'd be able to summarize the meetings easily. Boy, was I wrong! As I was taking notes at the first meeting, I recorded words that seemed familiar, but when I later tried to make sense of my notes for a summary, I realized that I was clueless about the specific meanings that the tax world used for these "ordinary" words!

How was I going to figure it out? After freaking out for a couple of days, with a bit of research I found a way to complete the summary. But I still remember the feeling of panic.

Now back to my plan for the teachers: I would read any section of the Income Tax Act to them. They wouldn't understand a thing -- even though I was reading English words. It was perfect!

I stood before them, saying that I had something important to share, randomly turning to a page in my thick book and started reading. As I droned on about non-arm's length transfers of assets, I saw them first look confused, then uncomfortable and finally ready to scream out of frustration and/or boredom.

I would eventually look up and ask if anyone could summarize the passage. Nope. What if I read it over again? Nope. What if I slowed down? Nope. Then came the final question: How many of you would become a behavioural problem if you had to listen to this every day without any way of understanding it? Several hands were raised.

If your classroom behaviour was not stellar, I understand. And I hope that you're feeling better about feeling different or less than the others.

There may be many reasons for acting out in class—and literacy gaps don't need to be one of them. That's why letter dis-order assessments and hands-on alphabet relearning should be an early step in ruling out this possible root cause for behaviour issues. As with Steven, it may also be the key for turning things around.

Myth Busting: Bullying

One day, I was in an unfamiliar school and was struggling to organize a class of students who had been sent to me without any teacher support. I was also on a deadline. I had two hours to prepare the students in this class to facilitate students in another class in a hands-on literacy event. Things were not looking good.

"I can help you, Ma'am." I turned around to see Samuel, a small, twelve-year-old boy, looking up at me. He stepped in and turned things around immediately. Not only did he organize and encourage his classmates to do their best, he showed them how to improve their delivery.

As a result of Samuel's help, the event was a great success.

After the students were gone and the classroom teacher finally(!) showed up, he was shocked to hear about Samuel's support. "Samuel spends more time in the principal's office for bullying than any other student in the school," he told me. All of his teachers feared his disruptions of their classes. He was considered to be a troublemaker.

Sure. That's probably what Samuel also believed. But everyone wants to feel important and will rise to the occasion when help is accepted or requested—even the so-called bullies.

Feelings of failure can unintentionally produce bullies and victims. It's for this reason that the best process for building literacy foundations not only prevents letter dis-order, it also creates an environment where learners support each other. Everyone wants to know that they matter and that they belong, especially when they learn differently. Samuel showed how, in the absence of negative expectations, one child's big energy can unify a group for a positive result.

Myth Busting: Low motivation

When I asked a few students to help me prepare clay ropes for a pilot project in their school, I did not expect the lunchtime "Rope Rolling Club" to become the hottest group in the school. Rather than play in the playground, students rushed to a line up that went around the corner in the hallway to sit at tables and roll clay into ropes. I repeat: rather than play outdoors, they chose to roll clay ropes for their teacher.

Why? They were hungry to contribute and feel that they matter. I was thrilled to have plenty of materials prepared for the 12 classrooms I visited every week. An unexpected benefit of inviting students to help: their motivation to do the activities in my literacy program significantly increased.

They say that a great way to encourage children to eat more vegetables is to have them grow and harvest them. If you want to engage students in a hands-on literacy program, let them roll clay ropes or contribute in some meaningful way and watch what happens with their motivation to apply the strategies!

Here's another example of how to boost motivation:
When I run workshops that include adults and children, it's amazing to watch what happens when the children pick up a skill that can help the adults do their work better. In one workshop, a seven year-old was the first to build a perfect "k" out of clay by using what we called a "k cut". As he went around the table showing the adults how to do their own k cuts, his confidence and enthusiasm soared!

Every person has a motivation hook and it often involves helping others succeed.

Myth Busting: Low skill level

Eleven-year-old Julian was struggling in school. He wore glasses, was bullied about being pudgy, couldn't read or write at grade level and struggled to learn things on his own. He was used to having his parents and older siblings help him with everything. As he consistently said that he couldn't do what was asked of him, it would have been easy to assume that even the simplest hands-on tasks to resolve letter dis-order were beyond his abilities.

When paired with a younger student who needed help with his alphabet relearning, however, Julian could suddenly explain and do things he couldn't do for himself. The connection and pride that came from supporting another person dissolved his own blocks.

Julian's generosity to another student reaped even greater benefits for himself as he overcame the limiting beliefs that were in his way.

Learning to read and write can feel daunting if everything you've tried before didn't work for you. Sometimes you just need the right team and partner to inspire your genius to show up for the literacy party.

Myth Busting: Individual versus group work

I was working with a group that included a seven-year-old boy and his mother. When it was time to do group work, we had one extra person when setting up the teams. I decided to work one-to-one with Jordan so that he would get more direct attention from me. As the teams had fun with their assignment I made sure that Jordan stayed on task while completing his work.

After finishing the first activity, Jordan asked if he could join a team for the next one. His mother volunteered her spot. While the teams were loudly laughing and supporting each other, Tina silently completed the task in record time, and then waited for the others to catch up.

Which way do you think Tina preferred to work?

Her response: it was satisfying to get the job done quickly, but it was way more fun to be on a team.

It may be faster when you do some work alone, but a group helps you feel connected and that you belong. In the right environment you feel compassion, patience and support for each other — and even for yourself. You realize that you're not alone.

You feel better about yourself than you have in a long time.

Supportive learning groups provide a wonderful human connection. You experience collaboration and kindness. You communicate with others; you play games that you can't play if you're alone. You discover talents you may not know you have. And besides, as Jordan and Tina will tell you, it's more fun.

Myth Busting: Testing proves learning

Teachers have a constant task of confirming that the lessons they teach are being learned. That's why they're always testing students. And when students are tested individually, it's easier to see what they know. That's why you may have done a lot of assignments and tests on your own. And you may have also felt alone if you ever failed.

How did you feel about tests? Where they easy, or stressful? Did you ever feel that you knew way more than you could show on your tests? I hope you can see by now how letter dis-order was playing a part in hiding what you really knew.

Is everything busted now?

Mahatma Gandhi said that the only way to remove darkness is with light. Hopefully, our myth busting helps to do just that.

I'm confident that letter dis-order is one of the most under-appreciated and misunderstood issues in literacy. In my experience, very few teachers have been taught about the signs of letter dis-order, its root causes, or the impact it has on their students. Even fewer know how to resolve the issue. That's why letter dis-order has a grip on too many people throughout their entire lifetime — making things way more difficult than they can be with a complete approach to literacy foundation.

"I was two years behind the rest of my class ...
I had to go through teasing and the teasing
led to a lot of other problems I had in school,
but it all stemmed from the fact that
I was embarrassed to stand up
in front of the class and read."

— Steven Spielberg,
Film Director, Producer and Screenwriter

CHAPTER 6

ASSESSING AND RESOLVING LETTER DIS-ORDER

Trey's mom Janet was worried that her fourteen-year-old son was weary of school. She supported him in every way she could, but he never seemed to do as well in school as his older brother and sister had. Plus, his writing was a mess and none of his teachers knew what to do about it.

After resolving his confusion, Trey turned things around — and his mother was thrilled that she could read her son's writing for the first time in his life. More importantly, she also saw a spark of confidence and enthusiasm in him that had been missing since he was six years old.

Like Trey, you might be looking for a way to turn things around. Or you may just want to learn something more about yourself, or resolve a nagging feeling you've always had about your literacy skills. Eliminate the issues behind your letter dis-order and watch what happens.

The best way to resolve letter dis-order is by using a holistic approach as you relearn the alphabet. Connect your eyes, hands, imagination and full body as the symbols make sense in new ways. You may even feel them in your body as a part of the process. This depth of clarity and certainty opens up new abilities in reading and writing. With certainty, confusion goes away, and challenges shift to proficiency.

The process begins best with alphabet assessments. They're a fascinating first step in moving toward alphabet confidence because most people don't realize that many problems start with their ABC's.

Like Oliver. Remember him? Nobody ever thought that he didn't know the alphabet. He was super bright but failing at writing and spelling. When asked to print out an upper and lower case alphabet, he couldn't recall any letters past the letter "L" in either case. Even singing *The Alphabet Song* didn't help. He missed three letters in his own name.

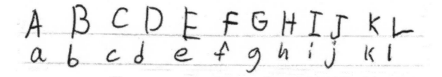

Alphabet assessments (without singing the song)

Below are the instructions for an alphabet assessment:

1. Print out the capital letters from A to Z.
2. Print out the small letters from a to z.
3. Draw a picture of anything you wish.
4. Write something about the picture.

Explanation:

1. and 2. The two alphabets reveal confusion about placement on the line, size, shape and spacing of each letter. Once we identify the points of confusion, we can start to resolve them. Sequence issues (including missing letters) also show up. In chapters 4, 5 and this chapter you can see examples of many assessments.

3. The drawing shows that you can control a pen. Sure, some letters show dis-order, but we see that you can control a pen to make a recognizable drawing. You don't have a fine motor skill issue that requires hours of tedious practice to correct.

If you're thinking: "But I suck at drawing." That's not the point. You don't need to be a Rembrandt to show that you can control a pen. You just need to draw something that resembles the subject you are drawing. Show that you're able to draw straight and curved lines.

4. It is also helpful to compare your printed alphabet with how you put your thoughts into writing.

Some people print an alphabet that looks pretty good on the surface but shows a lack of focus when writing out their thoughts. They never imagine that letter dis-order is distracting them and that it's affecting their writing.

Alphabet assessments provide a baseline to compare with improvements that emerge after the alphabet is relearned. The point is that until there is certainty with the alphabet, letter dis-order will exist in some way.

> "As a person with terrible handwriting, I love the computer. I've waited all my life for the computer."
>
> — Janet Fitch, Author

The type of assessment matters

It's also important for assessments to accurately uncover any confusion that exists. Here's an example of an alphabet sample when the student was asked to print out the upper and lower case alphabets:

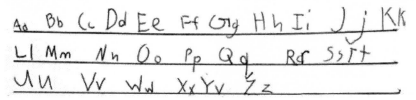

As the child was only seven years old, the parents were quite pleased with the result. Here's what was printed, however, when the student was asked to print out the upper and lower case alphabets separately:

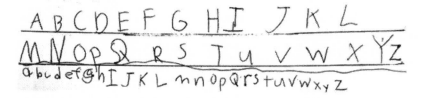

It was clear that classroom printing drills had combined the upper and lower case letters, making it appear that there was proficiency. Separating the two cases revealed another story.

Adults can be confused too

Even when adults are acutely aware of their reading and writing challenges they may not realize that letter dis-order exists and is impacting their lives. Assessments help to reveal the hidden causes of their issues.

This assessment shows an example of distracted writing:

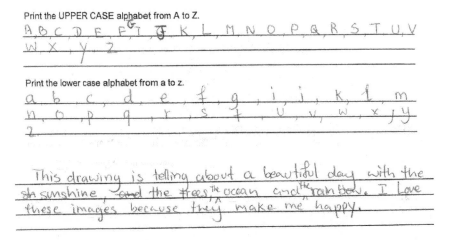

The adult who wrote the above sample didn't realize that both of her alphabets were missing a letter. Because her writing is neat, she would never suspect letter dis-order as one cause of her challenge to turn her thoughts into writing.

By the way, incomplete alphabets are not just a childhood problem. An adult provided this sample:

Are you talking about cursive or printed writing?

Alphabet relearning focuses on resolving confusion of printed letters (not cursive) for two reasons:

1. We read printed letters every day. We're looking at printed letters every time we read hard copy or digital books, forms, flyers, street signs, greeting cards, magazines, blogs, websites, and so on. Even the book you're reading right now. It's the same when we interact with digital media. Except for the odd time that we may see a fancy script style of font, most of the letters are in printed form.

Whole body learning of printed symbols deepens your connections to them. You'll read and write better. You'll also clean up messy writing. With certainty in your mind's eye about how each letter looks, and using your hands as part of the learning process, you're one step closer to training your hand to print letters that are in perfect order. Imagine having the freedom to choose when to print legibly for the first time in your life.

2. It's becoming rare for people to use cursive writing. I support any person's choice to use cursive writing — but I recommend gaining proficiency with printed letters as a first step for 21st century literacy. With a strong foundation in printed letters, cursive letters will be much easier to learn.

The return of cursive writing

Cursive writing is no longer compulsory in many countries as penmanship (the art of writing by hand) has lost its appeal, not only because it was time-consuming and didn't work for everyone, but because technology offered the alternatives of typewriters and computers. Students destined to have messy handwriting for life finally had a solution. Or so it seemed.

Have you ever run away from a problem, hoping it would resolve itself? Did it work out for you? Not here either. And because the underlying cause of letter dis-order was never addressed, 20–25% of students continued to fail on literacy tests.

So guess what? Cursive writing has recently been reintroduced into schools in more than 20 US states at both the primary and secondary levels. Good? Yes! Studies have shown many benefits to writing letters by hand. Necessary? I'm not really sure. Because those benefits apply to both printed and cursive writing, the renewed interest toward cursive may be misapplied.

The old way of teaching cursive was time-consuming and missed the mark for many. A simpler and more effective approach for teaching cursive writing — if you're determined to do it — is to focus on having a strong foundation with printed letters first.

Studies show that forming words by hand
(as opposed to using a keyboard):

- Leads to increased brain activity
- Increases your ability to focus and extend your attention span
- Improves long-term information retention
- Eases depression and anxiety by lightening your mood
- Slows down mental aging
- Causes better thought formation and understanding of material
- Increases creative ability to generate ideas

A solid printed-letter base that's taught with a growth mindset approach will lead to many powerful learning outcomes. It will also prevent confusion among those who really need a solid printed alphabet in their pocket before they add another version of letters to their letter options. (Are you listening, Louisiana, and the other cursive-seeking states?)

Who benefits from alphabet certainty?

One of the most important rules in marketing is to never say that your product is good for everyone. Marketing gurus will tell you that when you sell to everyone, you sell to no one. But here's what I've experienced: learning or relearning a solid foundation -- which for literacy includes alphabet certainty -- benefits everyone!

You may be one of those people who has always joked about your writing or spelling. Or you may say that it's "no big deal" because you use digital technology. The fact is, until you understand the root cause of your situation and learn to have command over it, you'll have nagging questions about it, either consciously or subconsciously.

Or, you may be someone who has legible writing but wishes it could be better. I used to be surprised when I would speak to groups about messy writing and the first people to ask for an assessment always had neat writing! I wondered why they were asking for assessments. I now see how the process enriches life-long learning for everyone -- even those with legible writing :-)

When you approach messy writing as an opportunity to learn and grow, it's quite easy to fix, and you'll have fun along the way. Here's the real benefit: The path to alphabet certainty enriches every person's ability to connect and communicate.

The new brain connections that grow during the learning process (neurogenesis) boost something in you. You'll read and write better, even if you were good at those things before.

Your awareness and focus also improve. And you feel smarter.

Let's look at a powerful and effective process for learning or relearning the alphabet that benefits all...

"Being dyslexic at school meant that I always liked to sit behind someone who wrote big."

— Richard Branson,
Entrepreneur and Author

To Certainty, and Beyond

"You never change things by fighting the existing reality.
To change something, build a new model that
makes the existing model obsolete."

— Buckminster Fuller,
Architect, System theorist, Author and Inventor

CHAPTER 7

IT'S TIME TO EDIT YOUR LIFE STORY

Let's do this together!

> "The illiterate of the 21st century
> will not be those who cannot read and write,
> they will be those who
> cannot learn, unlearn and relearn."
>
> —Alvin Toffler,
> Author and Futurist

When I first encountered this quote in 2006 (one of my all-time favourites), I thought Toffler was a genius. How could he have known how much faster the world would change in the future? He was so right. We had Wikipedia and a new thing called YouTube. Big things were happening.

As I complete this book in late 2022, I have to laugh: the changes of 2006 were slow compared to what the world has experienced since then, and especially over the past two years. And change will probably speed up even more in this century. That's why Toffler's form of resilience training --learn, unlearn, relearn-- is important to experience and practice.

I admit my bias as I say that I can't think of anything better to unlearn and relearn than the alphabet.

The alphabet is an efficient subject for relearning because, unlike some skills, it takes far fewer than 10,000 hours to master—only a few hours in fact. It can also offer unexpected benefits to every person.

Hopefully by now you appreciate the value of having certainty of these important communication symbols and are curious about how relearning them will impact your life. You'll soon see that it's not only important *that* you relearn them; *how* you relearn the letters is the key to high performance learning and resilience.

The ABCs of relearning your ABCs

Are you ready for more details about the mysterious process of replacing your current alphabet with one that's your "alphabest"? Great!

There are three stages: Learning Warm-ups, Tool-building, and Transformation.

Stage 1: Learning Warmups

Have you seen how athletes, martial artists and musicians warm up before practices, games and competitions? Athletes stretch muscles and practice shots. Singers prepare their vocal cords and musicians play scales before they perform. Professional speakers (including newscasters) also warm up their jaw, tongue and lips before speaking.

Why do they do these things?

They may believe that these rituals prepare them for success. And they may also understand that preparation of their brain and their body is a critical step into action!

What about learning warmups? Do you warm up to learn? If not, don't feel badly. Many learning specialists don't take time to prepare to learn. But when you think about it, doesn't it make sense? Before learning anything, warmups can improve your focus and help you better understand what you see, hear, feel and understand. These are simple actions that let you choose when to use your wild imagination to bend reality and when to be focused and oriented to the 3-D world in front of you.

When you signal to your brain that you want to succeed at an activity and do learning warmups, your brain will respond. Legible writing, good spelling and improved comprehension are coming your way. What's even better, these warmups can also help you perform better on tests, plus during interviews and presentations — even when making friends!

Your "Learning Warmups" actions are as follows:

1. Reflect on any times in your life that you have done any type of warmups. Are you an athlete or musician? Or do you warm up for another activity?

2. Imagine using warmups to grow your unique brain and body connections. What do you think would help your brain? As you use your personal warmup tools, you'll notice not only can you focus better, you'll feel better about everything in your life. Imagine feeling more confident about your skills in sports and connecting to others in new ways. How much more fun will life be when you know how to resolve your confusion and pay better attention?

Learning Warmups can be as simple as ABC --Allow, Breathe, Connect

If your learning experience has been one of working really hard and pushing through things that are confusing, how has it worked for you? Do you ever feel stress about learning new things? Do you ever get headaches or stomach aches in the process?

There is another way-- I call it "Allowing"

Allowing may sound weak, but it actually builds up your capacity to learn and succeed by using some simple actions for powerful results.

Allowing is about having a growth mindset—a phrase coined by renowned Stanford professor Carol Dweck.

Growth mindsets exist when you believe that your abilities and intelligence are not fixed. That is, you believe that when you use consistent effort and learn from feedback about your progress, your skills and results will improve.

You don't just sit back and expect things to come to you. You know that you will learn when you track your progress and use strategies that work well for you.

One great feature about growth mindsets is that you don't need to be born with them. Anyone can develop this approach to learning with the right environment and practice. This positive attitude also makes learning more interesting and fun! Imagine being curious about how to improve your outcome instead of just focusing on your score. Then you're free to experiment with different approaches until you find the one that works for you. That's growth mindset in action.

Within "Allow" there are three sub-actions: Assess, Believe and Commit.

Assess

When planning a trip, what important information do you need to know? First, you determine your starting point and your destination. Another factor is how you're going to get there: are you walking, driving or flying? Then you plan your route.

It's the same with your alphabet relearning adventure. Step one: find out where you are. The letter dis-order assessment described in chapter 6 works really well for establishing your alphabet starting point. It's a clear way to see where there is dis-order in your alphabet or writing sample. Once you know this, you can plan your ultimate destination or goal, and the best strategies for getting you there (the how).

The letter dis-order assessment is also valuable after relearning your alphabet. A new assessment will show you how far you have come in a short amount of time—and that it's celebration time!

Believe

Growth mindset makes things happen only when there's belief in your ability to succeed. And not just your belief, but also the belief of those around you. If, while in school, nobody (including yourself) had faith in your literacy skills, then it's not surprising that your foundation is incomplete.

What will it take for you to believe in your ability to transform into someone with legible writing, consistent focus and reading confidence? I know you can do it because I've seen it happen for so many people. How about you? Does reading about the success of others help you believe in yourself? Even a little bit? Just as a tiny key can unlock a massive door, let your first small belief open up your new dream story.

Commit

Because our world has become a giant distraction it can be a challenge to choose goals, not to mention achieve them. There are ways to improve the possibility that you'll meet your goals. First, choose and write down your goal. Why? When you write down a goal, you have a 40% chance of reaching it. When you share your goal with someone, the potential of reaching it will skyrocket to a whopping 80% chance of success. So tell someone —preferably someone who believes in you ;-)

Your "Allow" actions are as follows:

1. Reflect on beliefs about your literacy and learning skills. Did the myth-busting chapter shift your beliefs? Did it give you hope?

2. Write down your goal for resolving your challenges and share it with someone you trust.

After we "Allow" we "Breathe"

When you're learning something, you want your brain to openly receive the new information and have the necessary time and energy to organize it. Ideally, you're relaxed, alert, focused and confident. You want minimum distractions, especially ones that cause stress.

And then there's reality.

Remember how in Chapter 4 I said that learning and confusion go hand in hand? That confusion is inevitable when learning because otherwise you wouldn't be learning anything new? And sometimes it takes a long time to fully understand the new stuff, which can be frustrating or embarrassing—and stressful!?

Relax. Here comes breath to the rescue. Humans have known about the power of using the breath for improving our lives for millennia. For example, you can breathe one way to increase focus and energy, another way to help your brain process new information, and another to release stress that confusion can cause.

Your breath can be your secret learning tool because nobody else needs to know how or when you're using it. And when you learn to use your breathing according to different situations, your focus and other abilities will sky rocket!

Your "Breathe" actions are as follows:

1. Sit in a comfortable position and rest your hands on your lap. Make a fist with each hand as tightly as you can—squeeze until you can feel pressure all the way up to your elbows. Now let go—what you are feeling is a *release* of the pressure you just caused by squeezing your hands.

   Pressure can also be caused by your thoughts. When you feel confused, frustrated, afraid or angry, your body responds by making you alert to possible danger. Energy flows quickly in case you have to run or fight. Your brain shuts off everything except for simple, automatic responses. Good for quick responses, bad for higher level thinking and learning.

   The good news is that you can release this extra energy by using your breath. The even better news is that you can cause this release every time you feel pressure or want to refocus when your attention strays.

2. Take a deep breath in your nose and let it out your mouth while making a loud "ahh" sound. Try it again, touching the front of your neck. And again. Do you feel something? It's the vibration that causes the sound you're making and sends the release through the cells in your body.

   Now take a moment to pay attention to the space your fingers and toes are occupying in space. Breath in again and as you make the "ahh" sound, send the vibration all the way down to your fingers and toes. Keep repeating this until you feel a total release in your body. Make sure you're making a loud "ahh" sound as you do this, and don't be afraid to be too loud! Your body will thank you.

If you're thinking, "I can't do this when other people are around!" don't worry. This is the first step to feeling a release. Practice it in a private space if you'd like until you feel the flow of the release. Eventually you can achieve the same feeling just by sitting and breathing with an intention to release the stress.

3. Different breathing rhythms can help you either relax or add energy your body and brain as you warm up for learning. Each of the following forms of breathing is done through the nose, which is a very beneficial way to breathe.

   Balanced breathing—4 counts in through the nose, and 4 counts out through the nose—are a great way to relax your body and energize your brain at the same time. This rhythm is faster than we normally breath so it primes us to be alert for learning. Do this for 10 cycles of in/exhale to signal the brain and body that you're ready to learn.

   Quick exhales help to charge up your body when you're feeling that you need a boost. To do this, you'll exhale through your nose in a way that looks and feels like a sneeze. Relax your shoulders and quickly pull the belly in as you exhale through the nose. Try it for 20 exhales then relax the body and breathe normally through the nose. When ready, repeat 20 more quick exhales, relax, and again exhale 20X, for 3 rounds in total. This wakes up the sympathetic nervous system, which gives you the energy you require for fight or flight in dangerous situations—and an alert brain.

   Caution: limit the amount of times you do this during the day, because it can negatively affect your digestive system if you overdo it.

The "C" of the Warmup ABCs is for "Connect"

In Learning Warmups there are many ways for you to connect. You can connect to yourself, to other people, or to the situation in the room. All of these connections are important to help you be the best learner you can be.

Your "Connect" actions are as follows:

Remember that one important purpose of Learning Warmups is to set up your focus and orientation. You want to consistently see the letters in front of you so your brain can do its job of making patterns and keeping you safe! "Connect" actions bring it all together.

To begin, here's a practice for tuning in to yourself:

You can do this any time to relax and focus your entire body, either sitting in a chair or lying on your back.

- Close your eyes and wiggle your fingers and toes.
- Stop wiggling and notice how your fingers and toes feel. Do you feel warmth or tingling?
- Bring that feeling up to your knees and to your elbows (pause), then up to your hips and shoulders.
- Now move the feeling over your belly and chest and up your back. Pay attention to and relax your belly area.
- Feel your shoulders and allow them to release under the gentle weight of your arms.
- Move your awareness up your neck. Release your jaw as you separate your teeth.
- Soften your face, including your forehead, eyebrows eyelids, nose, cheeks and lips. Feel your eyes relaxing in their sockets.

- Move the softness around your scalp and ears.
- Bring your attention to your entire body, feeling the space you are occupying in space.
- Breathe gently.

There are many types of actions you can do any time to improve your focus. It may surprise you to learn that some repeated small movements done with your fingers and hands can help you improve focus and coordination:

Finger circles (sitting or standing)

- Make a fist with your thumb on the outside, keeping the index finger pointing straight up.
- Bend your elbows, keeping hands around shoulder height.
- Draw circles with your index fingers in outward circles. Start slowly and increase speed to go as fast as you can. Breathe slowly and deeply through your nose.
- Do each variation for 1-3 minutes. (longer session=greater focus)

  (Option: listen to a song and match the rhythm.)

Variations

- Circle your index fingers in inward circles.
- Circle your index fingers so that the right finger spins outward and left finger spins inward.
- Circle index fingers so that the left finger spins outward and right finger spins inward.
- Do all of these variations by circling your wrists, while pointing your index finger up!

Here's a fun way to connect with yourself and a partner — and feel certain that you're ready to learn:

Koosh Balls Note: for the full activity you learn to balance on one foot while throwing Koosh-style (rubber stringy) balls.

With Koosh balls you can level up your focusing skills and gain triple powers: by focusing on what you're doing, you become a better learner; by paying attention to your partner, you're being a great friend; and by coordinating your body's movements, you're growing athletic skills. Plus, you get to play with fun, colourful balls! How great is that?

Preparation

1. First, face your partner and move so that you're standing about 1.5 meters or 5 feet apart. (This distance gives you enough time to prepare to catch a ball when it's thrown to you, and is not so far that you have to throw the ball hard for it to reach your partner.)

2. Close your eyes and imagine that you're standing on one leg (you're actually still on two feet) and feeling very balanced. Pretend you're a tree, and feel roots growing from your feet and holding you firmly into the ground. As you are showing your brain what you want to accomplish, check to see what energy level will give you success, and set your energy to that level. Remember to breathe as you do this.

3. Now open your eyes and stand on one leg. Feel your roots holding you in balance. Allow your legs to touch each other lightly. If it is difficult to balance, close your eyes again and show your brain that you can balance in your imagination. Repeat this step until you can balance comfortably on one foot when your eyes are open.

4. *Single throws:* One partner begins as the throwing partner and holds two balls. As both partners stand on one foot, the partner who is holding the balls says, "I'm going to throw one ball; I want you to catch it with one hand. Are you ready?" Make eye contact with each other, and wait until the Receiver says, "Yes." The Throwing Partner will then gently throw a ball underhand, aiming for the middle waist area of their partner. The Receiving Partner will catch the ball in one hand. Remember that as the Thrower, your job is to help your partner succeed. Throw in an arc to give them time to make their catch.

5. The Throwing Partner will then say, "I am going to throw another ball; I want you to catch it with the other hand. Are you ready?" When the Receiver says, "Yes," the Throwing Partner throws the second ball in the same way as the first. The Receiver will catch the ball in the other hand.

6. Now, the Receiver is holding both balls and the roles reverse. Repeat the steps in the new roles.

7. If a ball is dropped or missed, the Receiver simply picks it up and keeps going. Repeat the throws and catches many times until you both can do this activity with ease.

Note: This game can be expanded with *Criss-Cross Throws* (e.g. throw a ball to left side of body and catch it with the right hand) or by *Throwing 2 Balls at One Time*, and catching one in each hand. When you can do all three types of throws and catches, your brain is focused and ready to learn!

And remember: Any time you want to check in on your focus and balance, simply balance on each foot for a short time and you'll know how you're doing. The body always tells the truth; all you have to do is ask and find your balance!

There you have it—learning warmups have three parts, and every action you take increases your potential for learning success. You'll notice that not only can you focus better, you also feel better about other things in your life. Imagine feeling more confident about your skills in sports and connecting to other people in new ways. How much more fun will life be when you know how to resolve confusion and pay better attention?

Stage 2: Build your tools

By now, you know that I'm obsessed with alphabet certainty. That's because I know that when you relearn the letters for a solid literacy foundation, your life will improve.

What I'm actually sharing with you is my passion for the all-phabet. What's the all-phabet?

It not only includes knowing:
- the letters forward and backward,
- every detail about each letter, including what parts are shared with other letters, and
- how to print every letter in order with respect to place, position and condition.

The all-phabet also includes:
- using focusing techniques that work for you,
- building a growth mindset,
- exploring as a team where everyone belongs,
- merging the sciences of learning and happiness, and
- feeling new confidence for lifelong learning and in your daily family, job and world experiences.

Speaking of all-phabets, let's have a look at one:

Aren't the letters interesting? They can also be life-changing.

Many people find that as they attach the pieces to form letters, they themselves become attached to their own alphabet! And for good reason: it's going to be the most beautiful and accurate alphabet you have ever made!

Alphabet certainty requires focus, imagination and your hands. The hands-on part includes making letters out of modelling clay and then playing a lot of games to learn the entire alphabet — forward and backward!

The process connects you to each letter in ways never before experienced. Some letters become special favourites. And the concrete feeling of "ownership" of something that was once a bunch of confusing symbols is empowering.

Once you've made your own alphabet in 3-D, there are many fun, active ways of connecting your hands, imagination and brain. Simply picking up and holding your letters can be surprisingly powerful. If you're like me, you may also feel a new brain and body connection for the first time.

Once when I was running pilot projects in schools, the School Superintendent dropped by. We invited her to feel the power of a hands-on experience. She picked up a student's letter "A" and held it in her hands until she could see it in her imagination. She said that she would always think of "A" in this new way and congratulated the student for her fantastic alphabet! Imagine how it felt for a student identified as a "slow learner" to have the Superintendent give that praise.

You never forget the letters you make because they are forever available in your imagination. You're also never confused about them, ever again.

CHAPTER 8

SO, GENIUS, HOW DO YOU FEEL NOW?

"Writing is difficult,
and I communicate this way very badly."

— Albert Einstein,
Theoretical Physicist,
Nobel Prize in Physics (1921)

Do you have a different story about yourself now? Does it make sense to you that your creative and smart brain has played a role in your confusion? Do you understand how the school system has come to influence your sense of self?

Do you believe that you ARE creative and smart?

Be patient. Your old beliefs have been around for a while. Your brain needs time to develop positive connnections between your new alphabet, reading and writing.

Beliefs are simply thoughts in our minds that we repeat — over and over again. Thinking new thoughts requires consistent effort. And your old stories have the power of repetition going for them.

Most of us find it much easier to believe what we see rather than imagine what we want to believe. That's why hands-on approaches can be helpful. If I tell you that you can write neatly in a matter of hours, you may or may not believe me. If you see it for yourself, however, you have no doubt. You may then be ready sooner to create a new story about yourself.

It also makes a big difference when you feel learning in your body through action, rather than just learning something in your head. With greater body awareness, you also learn to feel for yourself whether you actually understand something or you want to review it until you feel certainty. Do this for the rest of your life for fun, deep learning.

The world wants you; the world needs you

You may wish that you never had this challenge. You may wonder whether the pain of feeling stupid or lazy will ever go away. I want you (or someone you love and care about) to feel smart and creative as soon as possible. You matter. It's time to heal your wounds so that you have the confidence to seek more from yourself. Feel inspired as you continue to find out and express what makes you come alive. Have the courage to be you.

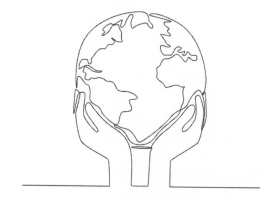

At the beginning of this book I asked you to appreciate your skill as a learner.

Top internet marketer Jason Fladlien asks this:

"How did you learn the most complicated technology on the planet with a poorly-developed brain and without an instruction manual?"

Of course he is talking about language — something so complex that even the experts in artificial intelligence programming can't duplicate it. And you learned your native language without going to school. You can even speak while doing other things such as walking, cooking or exercising!

Now, you also have information that's not known by many people, even though ideas about the importance of alphabet foundation have been around since the 1990's. The science is behind you to take on a model of learning that uses your talents and efforts in a positive way.

You can succeed as a reader, writer, thinker, and ultimately a lifelong learner who can confidently unlearn and relearn as the world around you changes.

So be ready and resilient.

The world wants your genius. Now!

"What sets you apart can sometimes
feel like a burden and it's not.
And a lot of the time, it's what makes you great."

— Emma Stone,
Actress

DEAR GENIUS

Yes, I'm talking to You

You, whose eyes betray the wounds
of being the bully or the bullied in the schoolyard.
Remembering to **this** day
the feeling of the pit in your stomach **that** day
when you gave the wrong answer in class,
and everybody laughed.

I hear what you think you can or cannot do
And what your third grade teacher sent home in notes
about your missing the brains, focus or effort boats.

It's time to cross the moat from that world
with your banner unfurled
and wearing the coat—of endless possibilities.

It's been many score that the
hallowed doors of learning have been my muse.
School may bore you
but I refuse to lose
my vision of genius for all who are bruised.

And in my cruise, this is what I've seen:

The 'truth" about learning is ever changing—
they keep re-arranging the stories
as the academy jostles for glory,
inventing new labels that pain and worry
—the cruelest form of allegory.

And changing nothing that really matters.

If reading or math cause stress,
or your writing's a mess
then you have yet to address
the critical basics for your learning success,
or be impressed by the value of knowing
some things with certainty.

Your foundation had cracks so you made your own hacks,
cheated or guessed, hid your shame to this day
in a game you weren't equipped to play.

But don't assign blame
we're all doing our best
caught in a system that is foundation-less
and focuses too much on the test.

Your stutter shows there's work to do
to find the true genius residing in you.

You choke on your words, desperate to be heard.

It may sound absurd, but here's the word:
The obstacle in your mouth starts in your head
and your dread of being misread
turns your tongue to lead.

They call you slow, but you're really too fast
to stay with the pack
and in your mind go back and forth
with thoughts and visions,
suffering derision because you don't go with their flow.

If they only knew what you know.
If there was time to explore
they could ask for more,
but the rush to "cover the curriculum" means that instead
you lie in you bed,
wondering "What's wrong with my head?"

There's nothing wrong with you!

You, who seeks only to accept and be accepted in love
but feel a need to succeed, to rise above, the others--
or fall behind.

It's not a race, sweet child of grace.
Their taste for haste exacerbates confusion
and comes from an illusion
of separation from the whole,
resulting in waste of your potential
as you play the wrong roles,
chase unfulfilling goals,
and eat from the bowl—of limitations.

It's time to get straight to the point of your greatness:
it's in you but you don't know it.
 You haven't learned how to consistently show it.

It's never too late to return to the gate
and lay a new foundation.

When you join the genius nation
you'll with focus and poise make an authentic noise
and claim your unique location with un-messable elation.

Stand up because you matter!
Without you the world would be flatter
and destiny's pattern would be missing a part.
You were born to make life your art
so start today to craft a new way.

I've got your back;
trust me with your heart.

Love, Your Soul

ABOUT THE AUTHOR

Diane Devenyi has taken a circuitous route to educational reform. After earning a law degree at Osgoode Hall Law School she began a career in taxation law. Motherhood shifted her priorities and by the time her second of three children was born she chose to pause her career to commit herself full-time to her family.

During this time she volunteered regularly in her children's schools, teaching reading, math and new computing skills. As her youngest child began full-time school, Diane prepared to return to work outside of the home but found herself drawn to learn more about improving the experience of education for the many students, teachers and families she saw who were struggling in the current educational system.

Fast forward twenty years of research, training and a return to graduate school to earn a Masters Degree in Education, Diane is the creator of online Wild Alphabet Adventures. She is also writing a series of books that merge the science of learning with happiness sciences — this being the first book of the series — and the author of the spoken word poems, Dear Genius and Education 3.0.

Diane is available for interviews and speaking engagements. To schedule time with Diane, or to find out more about her upcoming adventures, visit her website:

https://TheLearningForce.com/MeetDiane

CHAPTER TOPICS

Chapter Topics

YOUR NEXT STEPS:

To support your commitment to literacy, check out the free resources available at The Learning Force:

https://www.thelearningforce.com/resources

There, you'll find links for deeper dives into:

- Playing with order versus disorder
- Boosting growth mindset
- Improving focus and attention with fun challenges
- Decoding assessments
- And more (we keep adding to the list)

Wishing you a bright future of alphabet certainty and order!

"Onward and upward" — :-Diane

NOTES

Manufactured by Amazon.ca
Bolton, ON

32001617R00079